JENNIFER BERMAN

ADULT CHILDREN OF NORMAL PARENTS

ANNUAL CONVENTION

POCKET BOOKS

New York   London   Toronto   Sydney   Tokyo   Singapore

An Original Publication of POCKET BOOKS

POCKET BOOKS, a division of Simon & Schuster Inc.
1230 Ave. of the Americas, New York, NY 10020

Copyright © 1994 by Jennifer Berman
Cover illustrations by Jennifer Berman

All rights reserved, including the right to reproduce this book or portions
thereof in ANY FORM WHATSOEVER. For information address Pocket Books,
1230 Ave. of the Americas, New York, NY 10020

Library of Congress Catalog Card Number: 94-66805

ISBN: 0-671-86489-0

First Pocket Books trade paperback printing November 1994

10 9 8 7 6 5 4 3 2 1

POCKET and colophon are registered trademarks of Simon & Schuster, Inc.

Cover design by Tom Greensfelder

Printed in the U.S.A.

Many of the cartoons in this book have appeared as postcards
published by Humerus Cartoons. Being the lucky dog that you are,
you may write Jennifer for a catalog at Humerus Cartoons,
P.O. Box 6614, Evanston, IL 60204-6614.

DEDICATION

TO AL DENMAN, PATRON SAINT OF ANTIOCH COLLEGE, WHO ADVISED ME, IN HIS DECEPTIVELY SIMPLE WAY, TO FOLLOW MY HEART.

AND TO ANTIOCH ITSELF, FOR CONSISTENTLY ENCOURAGING DANGEROUS IDEAS.

ACKNOWLEDGEMINTS:

ORIGINAL CYNIC
BETCHA HE NEVER CALLS ME AGAIN, SNAKEY.
JENNIFER BERMAN ©1993

5

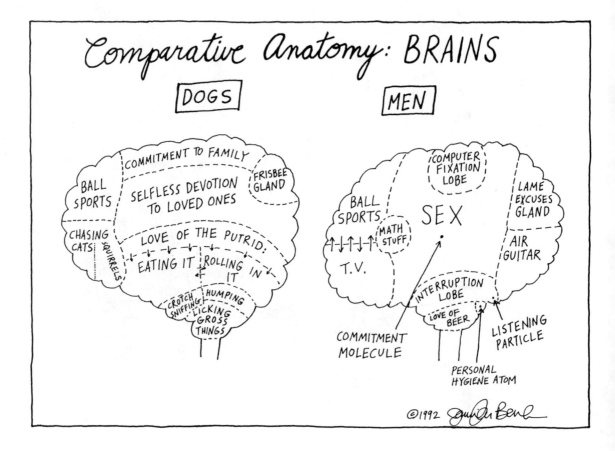

URBAN OWNERS OF
ALL-TERRAIN VEHICLES
DEFEND THEIR PURCHASES:

SOMETIMES WHEN IT RAINS REAL HARD, BIG PUDDLES FORM!

HEY– MY GIRLFRIEND'S GOTTA GRAVEL DRIVEWAY!

MY PORSCHE CLASHES WITH MY STONE-WASHED JEANS!

WE HAVE SOME TREACHEROUS CUL-DE-SACS RIGHT IN OUR NEIGHBORHOOD!

Berman ©1993

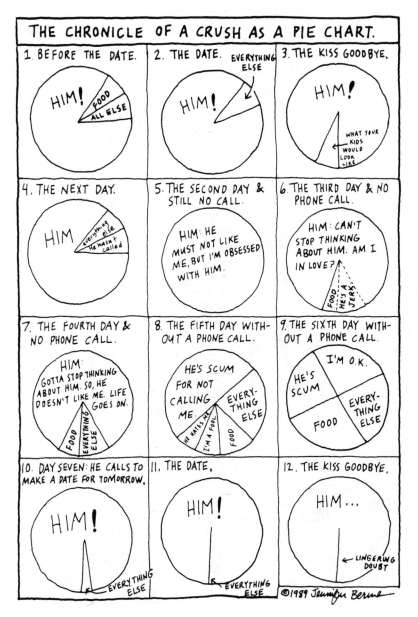

THE CHRONICLE OF A CRUSH AS A PIE CHART.

1. BEFORE THE DATE.
HIM! FOOD ALL ELSE

2. THE DATE.
EVERYTHING ELSE
HIM!

3. THE KISS GOODBYE.
HIM!
WHAT YOUR KIDS WOULD LOOK LIKE

4. THE NEXT DAY.
HIM
everything else
He hasn't called

5. THE SECOND DAY & STILL NO CALL.
HIM: HE MUST NOT LIKE ME, BUT I'M OBSESSED WITH HIM.

6. THE THIRD DAY & NO PHONE CALL.
HIM: CAN'T STOP THINKING ABOUT HIM. AM I IN LOVE?
FOOD HE'S A JERK

7. THE FOURTH DAY & NO PHONE CALL.
HIM: GOTTA STOP THINKING ABOUT HIM. SO, HE DOESN'T LIKE ME. LIFE GOES ON.
FOOD EVERYTHING ELSE

8. THE FIFTH DAY WITHOUT A PHONE CALL.
HE'S SCUM FOR NOT CALLING ME.
HE HATES ME I'M A FOOL FOOD EVERYTHING ELSE

9. THE SIXTH DAY WITHOUT A PHONE CALL.
HE'S SCUM I'M O.K.
FOOD EVERYTHING ELSE

10. DAY SEVEN: HE CALLS TO MAKE A DATE FOR TOMORROW.
HIM!
F EVERYTHING ELSE

11. THE DATE.
HIM!
E EVERYTHING ELSE

12. THE KISS GOODBYE.
HIM...
LINGERING DOUBT

©1989 Jennifer Berne

SELF-HARM BOOKS

DAILY DENIALS
365 PUT-DOWNS FOR EVERY DAY OF THE YEAR!

THE DRAMA OF THE STUPID CHILD

FAT IS A HOPELESS ISSUE

When Good Things Happen to BAD People

50 MORE THOUGHTLESS THINGS YOU CAN DO TO RUIN THE PLANET

WOMEN WHO LOVE TO ANALYZE TOO MUCH

Jennifer Berman ©1991

FATTENING FOOD
NEUTRALIZERS

BURGER & FRIES → LARGE DIET SODA

CHEESECAKE → CITRUS SPARKLING WATER

LINGUINE IN CREAM SAUCE → PLAIN SALAD

©1991

IS THAT **OVERFLOWING EGO** CAUSING UNSIGHTLY MISHAPS?

IS HE JUST TOO SELF-CENTERED FOR HIS OWN GOOD, AND THE SAFETY OF LOVED ONES NEARBY?

TRY NEW **MANPAX!**™ SIGHTLESS. ODORLESS. DISCREET. WILL MAKE HIM APPEAR TO ACTUALLY THINK OF OTHERS!

SIMPLY INSERT IN HIS EGO, AND GO!

- SWIM! • PLAY COMPETITIVE SPORTS!
- ARGUE with the confidence of knowing you may be wrong AND YOU'LL SURVIVE!
- NOW YOU CAN EVEN GIVE IN!

BEFORE — AFTER

ME ME ME ME ME ME ME ME ME ME ME ME ME ME ME ME ME ME ME ME ME ME ME ME ME ME ME ME ME ME ME ME ME ME ME ME ME ME ME ME ME ME ME ME ME ME ME ME

HOW ARE YOU?

ACTUAL CARTOONS.

USED REGULARLY, THE MANPAX ™ MAN WILL ACTUALLY ASK YOU QUESTIONS!

READ INSIDE WARNING ABOUT TOXIC SCHMUCK SYNDROME

MANPAX

BRAWNY HE-MAN SMELL!

FLUSHABLE IMPLICATOR

Ego-Degradable

DISCREET WALLET-PAC ENCLOSED

40

SUPER SELF-ABSORBENT

3 STYLES: SELF-ABSORBENT SUPER SELF-ABSORBENT and MAMMOTH IVY-LEAGUE HUNGRY-EGO

© 1991

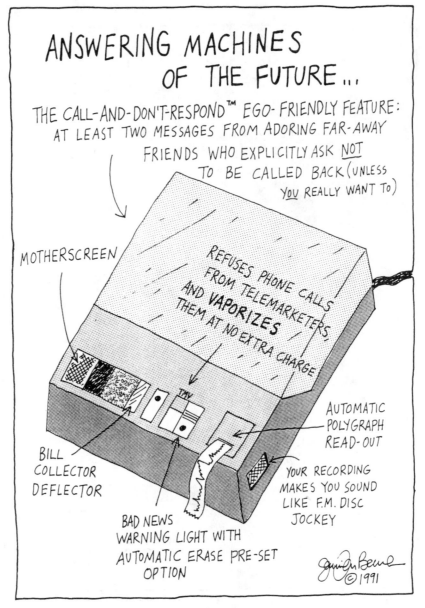

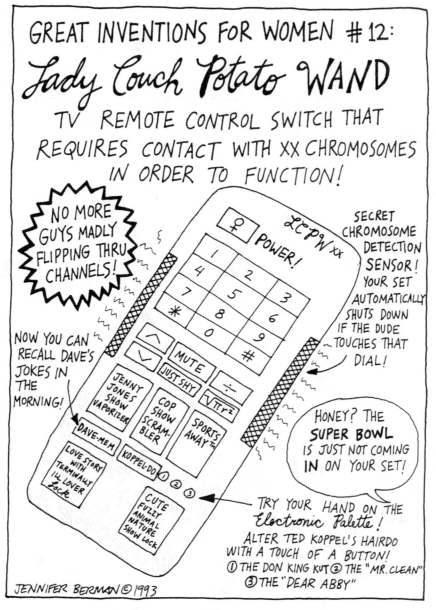

GREAT INVENTIONS FOR WOMEN #12:

Lady Couch Potato WAND

TV REMOTE CONTROL SWITCH THAT REQUIRES CONTACT WITH XX CHROMOSOMES IN ORDER TO FUNCTION!

NO MORE GUYS MADLY FLIPPING THRU CHANNELS!

SECRET CHROMOSOME DETECTION SENSOR! YOUR SET AUTOMATICALLY SHUTS DOWN IF THE DUDE TOUCHES THAT DIAL!

NOW YOU CAN RECALL DAVE'S JOKES IN THE MORNING!

POWER!

LCPW xx

DAVE-MEM
JENNY JONES SHOW VAPORIZER
COP SHOW SCRAMBLER
SPORTS AWAY™
LOVE STORY WITH TERMINALLY ILL LOVER Lock
KOPPEL-DO
CUTE FUZZY ANIMAL NATURE SHOW LOCK
JUST SHY
MUTE

HONEY? THE **SUPER BOWL** IS JUST NOT COMING **IN** ON YOUR SET!

TRY YOUR HAND ON THE *Electronic Palette*! ALTER TED KOPPEL'S HAIRDO WITH A TOUCH OF A BUTTON! ① THE DON KING KUT ② THE "MR. CLEAN" ③ THE "DEAR ABBY"

JENNIFER BERMAN © 1993

31

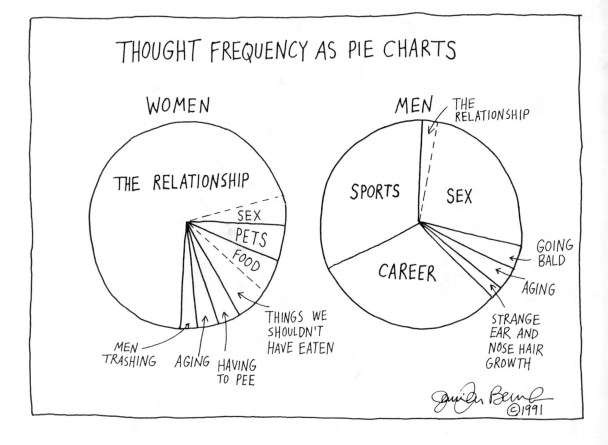

THOUGHT FREQUENCY AS PIE CHARTS

WOMEN

THE RELATIONSHIP

SEX
PETS
FOOD

MEN TRASHING   AGING   HAVING TO PEE

THINGS WE SHOULDN'T HAVE EATEN

MEN   THE RELATIONSHIP

SPORTS   SEX

CAREER

GOING BALD

AGING

STRANGE EAR AND NOSE HAIR GROWTH

©1991

HEY, GALS! TRY THE

ICKY MAN SHUFFLE!

IT'S EASY! IT'S FUN! AND IT'S THE ONLY GAME IN TOWN!

1. MEET NEW MAN.

2. CONVINCE YOURSELF HE'S WONDERFUL; FIND HIS FAULTS ENDEARING.

3. FALL IN LOVE....

SEAT UP, OF COURSE

4. ....THEN FIND OUT HE'S INCAPABLE OF LOVING YOU.

silent

5. THIS TAKES A LONG TIME TO SINK IN.

6. GET REALLY HURT. CRY A LOT.

7. BORE & ANNOY YOUR FRIENDS WITH WEEK AFTER ENDLESS WEEK OF IRRATIONAL SADNESS OVER LOSS OF FRIENDSHIP YOU NEVER REALLY HAD.

OH, YOU DON'T SAY

Friend on end of rope with you.

8. ALL OF A SUDDEN, SEE YOUR SITUATION FOR WHAT IT IS, FEEL LIKE A FOOL FOR EVER HAVING LOVED HIM. GET OVER HIM.

DINK!

9. SWEAR OFF EVER HAVING ANOTHER RELATIONSHIP.

THE NEW YOU?

10. REPEAT.

© 1990 JENNIFER BERMAN

36

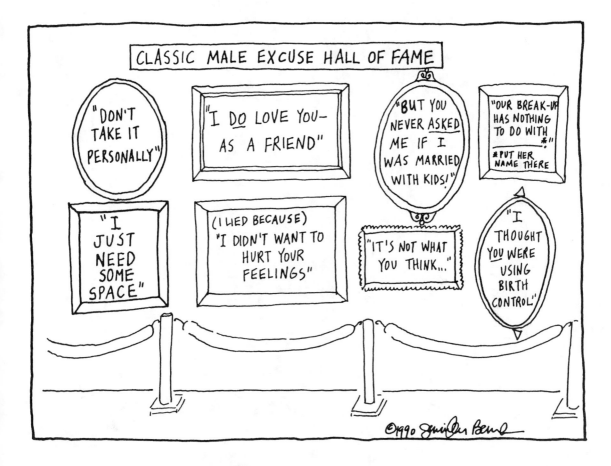

HEY, GALS! BAFFLED BY YOUR BEAU?
YOU'RE NOT STILL TAKING HIM LITERALLY, ARE YOU?
BURLITZ PROUDLY PRESENTS
OH, NO!
SAY IT IN GUY!

BEFORE RELATIONSHIP		DURING RELATIONSHIP		AFTER RELATIONSHIP	
GUY	ENGLISH	GUY	ENGLISH	GUY	ENGLISH
YOU'RE THE MOST FASCINATING WOMAN I'VE EVER MET	I THINK I'D LIKE TO GET INTO YOUR PANTS	I LOVE YOU MORE THAN ANY HUMAN HAS LOVED ANY OTHER HUMAN	I LOVE GETTING INTO YOUR PANTS ON A REGULAR BASIS	I NEVER REALLY LOVED YOU	THANK YOU FOR LETTING ME INTO YOUR PANTS
YOU'RE THE MOST BEAUTIFUL WOMAN I'VE EVER MET	MAY I PLEASE GET INTO YOUR PANTS NOW?	I LOVE YOU MORE THAN THE WORLD SERIES	I AM A PATHOLOGICAL LIAR	LET'S JUST BE FRIENDS	I HAVE GOTTEN INTO SOMEONE ELSE'S PANTS
YOU ARE MY SPIRITUAL TWIN	HOW ABOUT NOW?	I'LL CALL YOU SOON	I'LL CALL YOU WHEN I NEED SOMETHING	OUR FRIENDSHIP IS VERY IMPORTANT TO ME	PLEASE INTRODUCE ME TO YOUR GIRLFRIENDS

REMEMBER, SPEAKING TWO DIFFERENT LANGUAGES CAN ONLY SPELL DISASTER. LEARN GUY. TODAY. ©1992

THE HALF-WAY DECENT MAN

49

IN LOVE : OUT of LOVE

In Love:
- incredibly creative
- loves his family
- brilliant in his field
- sensitive
- totally charming
- tells you you're wonderful
- tells you you're special...
- Holds politically correct views
- One of the best men you've ever met

Out of Love:
- sociopathically manipulative
- has shrine to his mother in his bedroom
- obsessed with work to exclusion of all else
- ...to his own selfish needs
- liar
- ...so you'll let him get away with murder
- ...just like every other female in the universe
- ...as long as he doesn't have to act on them
- tragically, this is still true...

©1990 Jennifer Berman

I LIKE MY COFFEE
BLEAK

~OR~

GROUNDS FOR DISMISSAL
a short story/long cartoon

TWO BLISSFUL YEARS SAIL BY. ON THE NIGHT OF OUR SECOND ANNIVERSARY WE HAVE A ROMANTIC DINNER AT OUR FAVORITE THAI RESTAURANT AND HE BRINGS ME A STUNNINGLY BEAUTIFUL BOUQUET OF WILDFLOWERS. WE'RE SO ENRAPTURED THAT WE SKIP DESSERT AND HIGH-TAIL IT HOME TO OUR BEDROOM.

IN THE MORNING I REALIZE THAT MY TRUSTY OL' DIAPHRAGM HAD BECOME DISLODGED.

A COUPLE NERVOUS WEEKS PASS. MY PERIOD DOES NOT COME.

I TRY EACH BRAND OF PREGNANCY TEST, ALL OF WHICH TURN THE LITTLE STICKS OF PLASTIC THAT UNDENIABLE YOU'RE-PREGNANT BLUE.

TEARS OF JOY AND TORRENTS OF FEAR WILL WASH OVER US FOR WEEKS, BUT ULTIMATELY WE FEEL OVERWHELMINGLY EXCITED ABOUT BEING PARENTS. IT WILL BE AN EASY PREGNANCY. AFTER NINE MONTHS AND THREE DAYS, I, WITH THE LOVING SUPPORT OF MY HUSBAND AND MIDWIFE (WHO, BEFORE THE 30 HOURS OF LABOR, WAS MY BEST FRIEND), GIVE BIRTH TO A BOY. WE NAME HIM JOSEPH, BECAUSE WE BOTH HAD REALLY COOL GREAT UNCLES NAMED JOE. MINE FOUGHT IN THE FRENCH RESISTANCE, HIS IS AN ANCIENT, CRUSTY LONGSHOREMAN UNION ORGANIZER. THE LAST NAME DILEMMA IS SOLVED BY THE SOLOMONIC FLIPPING OF A COIN... BUT THE NEXT BIG DECISION RESULTS IN OUR FIRST HUGE BLOW-OUT FIGHT...

HAVING MY BABY...

STOP!

BRING ON THE FUDGE—IT'S AN EMERGENCY!

Heads, I win, Tails, you lose, ok?

OK. NO. WAIT!

WAR and PEAS

IN THE END, I WIN — BUT THE ARGUMENT MARKS THE FIRST OF MANY FUNDAMENTAL DISAGREEMENTS. OVER THE YEARS JOE BECOMES THE BATTLEGROUND FOR ALL OF OUR POWER STRUGGLES. AS HE GROWS OLDER HE COMES TO RESENT US DEEPLY FOR MAKING HIM THE PAWN IN OUR CHECKERED MARRIAGE.

C'MON, SON — I GOT FRONT ROW SEATS TO THE WORLD SERIES!

JOE, AUNT FREIDA'S HAVING A BRUNCH, AND SHE'S FEELING SO ILL, THIS MIGHT BE YOUR LAST CHANCE TO SEE HER.

WHILE HIS FRIENDS ADORE HIS CONCILIATORY NATURE, JOEY WILL SEEK OUT A THERAPIST TO HELP HIM RELINQUISH HIS CHRONIC AND UNDESIRED ROLE AS PEACE-MAKER.

WE SPEND THE REST OF OUR LIVES TOGETHER
FEELING BITTER, WOUNDED & BETRAYED, STAYING MARRIED
ONLY BECAUSE OUR FEAR OF BEING ALONE OUTWEIGHS OUR
MUTUAL CONTEMPT.

SLURP!

MUST YOU ALWAYS SLURP YOUR FOOD?!

BUT IT'S SPAGHETTI— YOU'RE SUPPOSED TO SLURP IT!

THEN, IN HIS LATE SIXTIES, HE DIES OF A HEART ATTACK.
LEAVING ME ALONE AND WRACKED WITH GUILT, I HAVE VERY
LITTLE TO SHOW FOR MY LIFE—JUST AN UNICIRCUMCISED SON
WHO RESENTS ME, A HORRIBLE LONGING FOR MY DEPARTED
SPOUSE, AND ROSY REVISIONIST MEMORIES OF OUR
MISERABLE LIFE TOGETHER.
WITHOUT MY UNGRATEFUL MATE TO FEED,
I QUICKLY LOSE INTEREST IN COOKING
AND EATING. BEFORE LONG I BECOME
NOTHING MORE THAN A DESICCATED
PILE OF TEETH, BONES AND HAIR.